Musical Instruments

DENYS DARLOW

A & C · BLACK LTD
LONDON

Black's Junior Reference Books

General Editor: R. J. Unstead

© 1968 A. & C. BLACK LTD
FIRST EDITION 1962
SECOND EDITION 1968
REPRINTED 1970 AND 1972
ISBN: 0 7136 0113 2

PUBLISHED BY A. & C. BLACK LTD
4, 5 & 6 SOHO SQUARE, LONDON W1V 6AD

MADE IN GREAT BRITAIN
PRINTED BY MORRISON AND GIBB LTD., LONDON AND EDINBURGH

Contents

The instruments played by these mediaeval minstrels are the tabor and pipe, triangle, shawm, trumpet, harp, lute, bagpipes, psaltery, bombard and portable organ.

Acknowledgments

The illustrations in this book are by John Lawrence and Charles Gorbing-King. The photograph on the cover is reproduced by kind permission of Robert Freson and the *Sunday Times*.

Grateful acknowledgment is made to the following for permission to reproduce photographs : Boosey and Hawkes, pages 15, 21, 24, 26, 31, 33, 34, 35, 36, 54, 56, 62 ; British Broadcasting Corporation, pages 26, 57, 65 ; British Museum, pages 4, 22, 49, 53 ; British Travel and Holidays Association, pages 13, 31, 56; Daily Mirror, page 21; Fox Photos, pages 33, 43 ; Griffith Institute, Ashmolean Museum, Oxford, page 7 ; Henry Grant, pages 5, 39, 43; E. Hoppé, page 47; Horniman Museum, page 32 ; Keystone Press, pages 25, 42 ; London County Council, page 17 ; Mansell Collection, pages 14, 58, 59 ; Philharmonic Orchestra, page 9 ; Paul Popper, pages 22, 71, 75 ; Pictorial Press, page 42 ; Radio Times Hulton Picture Library, pages 8, 21, 27, 28, 35, 43, 55, 63; Spanish Embassy, page 52.

Illustrations on pages 24, 29, 44, 50, 51, 61, 66, 67, 68, 69 and 74 are from A. J. Hipkins' *Musical Instruments* (A. & C. Black) ; and the drawings on pages 20, 48, 53 and 69 are from Mary Houston's *Ancient Egyptian, Mesopotamian and Persian Costume* and *Mediaeval Costume in England and France* (A. & C. Black).

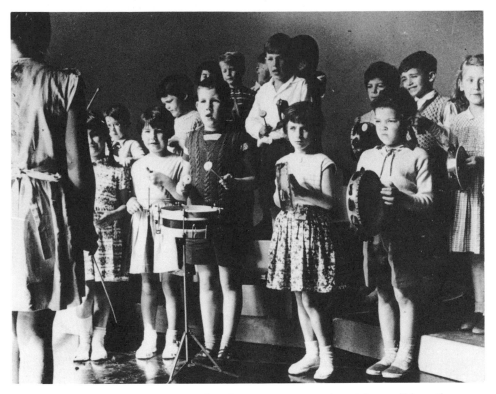

A percussion band. Percussion instruments are played by striking them.

1. Introduction

All musicians, except singers, need a musical instrument; this book tells you about these instruments in the hope that, when you have read it, you will enjoy music with more understanding.

Today over 50 different musical instruments are in general use. They can be divided into five groups:

> Strings
> Wood-wind
> Brass
> Percussion
> Keyboard

All the instruments in each group have something in common which gives the group its name. String instruments have strings on them to produce the sound; wood-wind instruments are made of wood, and the wind, or breath, is used to play them; brass instruments are made of brass; percussion instruments get their name from the word *percuss* which means "to strike"; and, lastly, the keys which are grouped together to form a keyboard, give the keyboard instruments their name.

But there are exceptions. You will read later that some of the wood-wind instruments can be made of metal or plastic.

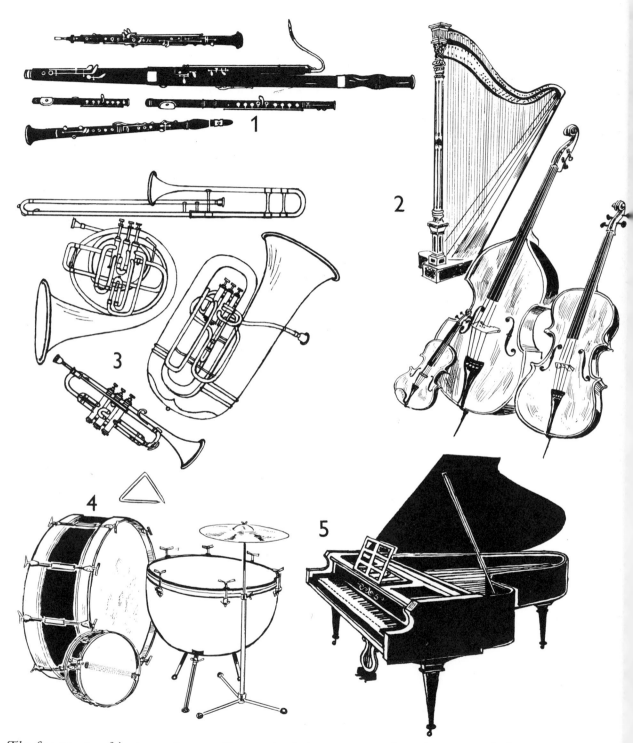

The five groups of instruments : 1. the wood-wind group ; 2. the strings ; 3. the brass group ; 4. percussion, and 5. keyboard instruments

Bow

DOUBLE BASS

PICCOLO

Each instrument in these groups has its own special personality, or, to put it in another way, its *tone-colour* or sound. Each has its own range of notes, or *compass*, and its special method of being played.

In all groups there are both small and large instruments, with many sizes in between. It is important to notice the size of the instrument, as this affects the *pitch* of the note. Small instruments sound high notes, large ones sound low notes and medium-sized ones make middle notes.

Many of the instruments have a long ancestry. For example, the trumpet's ancestors were known to the Ancient Egyptians, and the flute to the Greeks of Socrates' time in 400 B.C. Two verses from the Psalms remind us of the early instruments :

"With trumpets also and shawms,
O shew yourselves joyful."

and

"Take the psalm, bring hither the tabret : the merry harp with the lute."

Today, the sounds as well as the names of many of the ancient instruments have almost been forgotten.

The piccolo sounds high notes because it is a small instrument, the double bass sounds low notes because it is a large instrument.

This has happened because, as modern instruments developed from older ones, they received many improvements and changes of name.

A modern symphony orchestra has as many as 80 players, who use a great variety of instruments, some from each of the five groups.

An Ancient Egyptian trumpet in use about 1350 B.C.

7

Introduction

An orchestra in the eighteenth century. Frederick the Great is playing the solo flute part, accompanied by five court musicians with two violins, viola, 'cello and harpsichord.

But although the orchestra may have 80 players, they will not be playing 80 different instruments. In the string section, for instance, only four different instruments are used—the violin, viola, 'cello and double bass—and these are played by perhaps half the orchestra. There may be 12 first violins, 10 second violins, 8 violas, 6 'cellos and 4 double basses. Similarly, in the wind and percussion departments, there is more than one of many of the instruments.

Orchestras can vary in size and variety, depending upon the needs of the composer. For example, some composers require the strings alone, others strings with 2 oboes and 2 horns. Bach sometimes composed for strings, 3 oboes, 2 bassoons, 3 trumpets, 2 drums, harpsichord and organ. Brahms, in one of his serenades, wanted only the lower strings—violas, 'cellos and double basses, with 2 flutes, 2 oboes, 2 clarinets, 2 bassoons and 2 horns.

If you look at the score of a symphony—a *score* is a copy of the complete music as distinct from a *part* which is played by one performer—you will notice that the instruments are set out in a special order. At the top of the page are the wood-wind parts, each instrument or pair of instruments on a separate line ; next the brass and percussion, and finally the strings. If there is a keyboard instrument or harp in the orchestra, the part is usually printed between the percussion and strings.

8

A modern orchestra (The Royal Philharmonic). Each instrument or group of instruments is named in the diagram below.

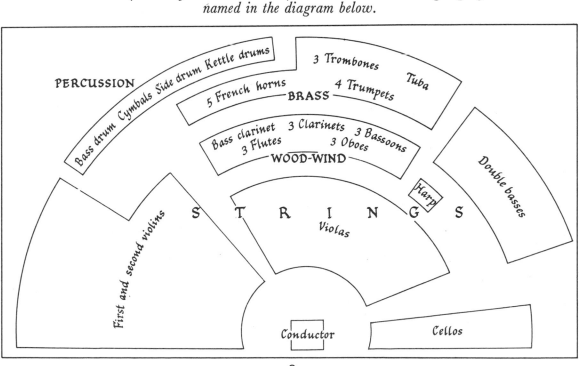

2. Wood-wind Instruments

You know that if you blow in a certain way into a fountain-pen top or an empty lemonade bottle, you can make a note, though it may not be very musical. This happens because you have made the air inside vibrate or quiver. In the same way, the player of a wood-wind instrument causes the air inside a tube to vibrate. Later, you will read how this happens to each instrument.

A long tube will sound a low note, a short tube a high note. If one tube sounds one note, how do we get lots of notes from a wood-wind instrument to make a tune?

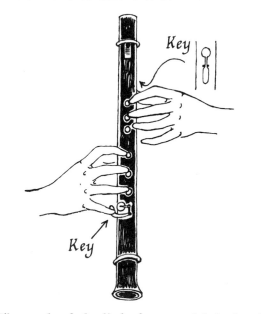

The work of the little finger and left thumb was made easier by adding keys.

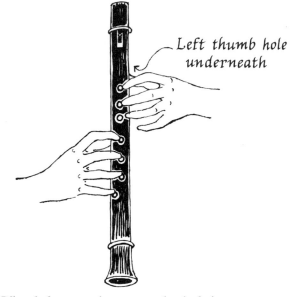

The holes cut in a wood-wind instrument alter the length of the tube to produce high and low notes.

This is done by cutting small holes at special places in the tube. When these holes are covered by the fingers, the player is using the whole length of the tube ; if he raises a finger and uncovers a hole, he has in effect made the tube shorter. The instrument now produces a higher note.

By this method the bassoon, which is long, can be shortened so that it is the same length as the oboe or flute. When the instruments become the same length, the note they sound will be the same. Because of this, one wood-wind instrument can play many of the notes of another.

Eight original holes numbered

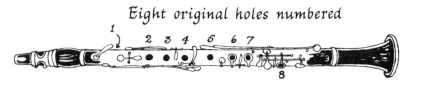

Simple key system (Clarinet)

Other keys were added so that notes that required difficult finger-work could be played more easily.

Early wood-wind instruments had eight holes. The middle three fingers of each hand covered six holes, the left thumb and right little finger the other two holes. You will notice that, owing to the shortness of the little finger, the bottom hole is cut a little to one side. The awkwardness of using this finger and the necessity of placing it in exactly the correct position made its task difficult. Many early instrument makers were aware of this and fitted a key to do the job of the little finger. All that now remained for the finger to do was to press the key. The left thumb, too, had some difficulty and a similar key was fitted.

On many instruments certain notes required a very difficult fingering and most of them had trills that could not be played at all. (A trill consists of two notes next to each other played alternately either very quickly or slowly.) These problems caused the instrument makers to experiment with additional keys and systems of keys.

Over the years, they have perfected a system of key-work which, with a few extra holes, has been built around the original eight holes and has cured many of the faults and difficulties. One of the most famous of the inventors of key-work systems was Boehm.

All the additions, varying with each instrument, have resulted in the modern versions that you see in the pictures, and the additional keys are so placed that the fingers can work them with ease and speed.

With the exception of the flute family, wood-wind instruments are *reed instruments*. The *reed* is a separate device which is fixed to a special part of the instrument. It is the means by which the air inside the instrument is made to vibrate. The clarinet and saxophone are the only wood-wind instruments requiring a single reed. All the others require two, and are sometimes known as *double-reed instruments*. They are the oboe, oboe d'amore, cor anglais, bassoon and contra bassoon.

Wood-wind Instruments

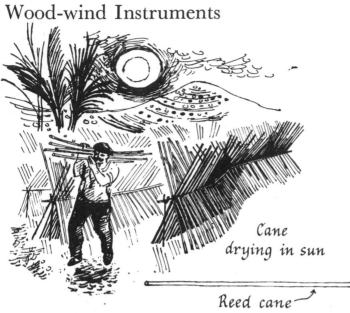

Cane drying in sun

Reed cane

Much of the cane from which the reeds are made is grown in the south of France.

The muscles of the lips which are used for forming the *embouchure* soon become tired, and for this reason wind players like to rest before a concert. (The word embouchure means the way in which the lips are applied to the mouthpiece of the instrument or the way in which the lips are used). If a player's " lip has gone ", an expression used by wind players, it is almost impossible to play.

The reeds are made from green cane which grows in the Mediterranean countries. The reeds must be carefully selected, shaped, and shaved down as thin as newspaper.

Although there are manufacturers of reeds, many players still prefer to make their own.

A good reed is vital to all players of reed instruments. A bad one can produce a poor tone or cause difficulties for the player by breaking in the middle of an important solo passage. It is by far the most sensitive part of his instrument and the most unreliable. All players carry a box of spare reeds with them, and it is not uncommon to see a player change a reed during a musical performance.

Some boys and girls will know already how difficult it is to control the vibrations of the reed with the lips, but those who are thinking of learning a wind instrument need not be discouraged by this difficulty. The lungs and the lips soon get used to the demands imposed on them.

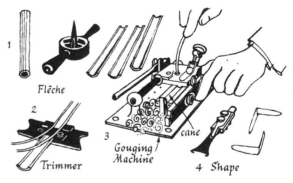

1 *Flèche*

2 *Trimmer*

3 *Gouging Machine* *cane*

4 *Shape*

1. Splitting the stick of cane into strips with the flèche.
2. Trimming the sides of the strip of cane.
3. Gouging the cane on the inside.
4. Shaping the sides of the bent-over cane to the shape of the reed.

Stages in the making of a reed

The wood-wind section of an orchestra. Front row : piccolo, two flutes, two oboes, cor anglais. Second row : bass clarinet, two clarinets, three bassoons.
(the five men in the back row are playing brass instruments)

Most composers allow plenty of rests for the wind instruments, particularly before solo passages. Not only does this give the player's lips and lungs a rest, but it draws attention to the instrument when it does enter.

The wood-wind group of Beethoven's time consisted of 2 flutes, 2 oboes, 2 clarinets and 2 bassoons. This is an ideal arrangement, as the 4 primary wood-wind tone-colours are represented. Any wood-wind instrument added to this group will belong to one of the 4 families and will have the same tone-colour as the family to which it belongs.

The wood-wind group of the modern full orchestra consists of :

2 flutes	piccolo
2 oboes	cor anglais
2 clarinets	bass clarinet
2 bassoons	contra bassoon

Many composers use a much smaller wood-wind section than this.

Mozart sometimes used only 2 oboes and 2 horns as his complete wind section. Later composers, such as Richard Strauss and Vaughan Williams, have used more than the usual number of instruments, including the oboe d'amore and saxophone.

The main purpose of the additional instruments, apart from their own special character, is to increase the range of their own particular family. For example, the piccolo plays higher notes than the flute, and the alto flute plays lower notes, the tone-colour being essentially the same for the three instruments.

Wood-wind Instruments

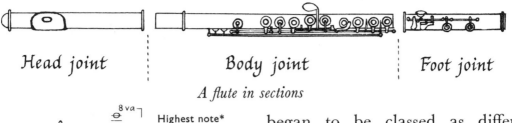

| Head joint | Body joint | Foot joint |

A flute in sections

Flute

Highest note*
Lowest note*

Metal, ebonite or hardwood. Length : $26\frac{1}{2}$ in. approx.

The ancestors of the flute can be traced back to the days of primitive man when he used a pipe or kind of flute for his religious ceremonies.

At a later period of history a flute was one of two kinds, a long-blown flute (recorder) or a cross-blown flute (transverse flute), depending on the way in which it was played. Although both types are members of the same family, at some time they began to be classed as different instruments. In some royal documents of the year 1543 a reference is made to recorder players and flute players. Purcell is referred to as a " keeper, maker, mender and tuner of flutes, recorders and other kinds of musical instruments ".

The orchestral flute is easily remembered, apart from the sound, by the way in which it is held. It is the cross-blown flute and is held across the player's mouth. This type of flute came into more general use about the year 1750.

Normally, the flute is made in three sections : the head joint, with the mouth-hole cut in the side ; the body or middle joint, with the main key-work ; and the foot joint, with the key-work for the right little finger. Sometimes the last two joints are made in one piece, but the head joint is always separate. These three sections slot together quite easily and for the purpose of tuning, which is often necessary due to the instrument's change in pitch through heat, the head joint can be pulled out on a special slide.

* All the other notes between these two can be played. The range or compass of the other instruments is also given in this way.

A singer of the sixteenth century accompanied by transverse flute and lute

The embouchure of the flute, or the way in which the lips are applied to the mouth-piece of the instrument

The mouth-hole is placed just under the player's bottom lip. As the player's breath leaves his mouth, directed in a thin stream against the far side of the mouth-hole, small whirl-pools which form in the air flutter rapidly and cause the air inside the flute to vibrate and sound a note.

The top notes of the flute sound very bright and clear, the low notes softer and less penetrating. Sometimes these low notes can be mistaken for distant trumpets and this is an effect often used by composers. Bright cheerful tunes are usually given to the flute, also quick passages and tunes that jump about. Although bright tunes fit the character of the flute especially well, composers sometimes give it slow and more lyrical tunes to play. These sound very beautiful and show another side of the flute's "personality".

Metal flutes are now the most popular, although plenty of players still prefer wooden flutes. Mass-produced metal flutes can cost £30

to £40; a better instrument, of wood or metal, will cost as much as £160 to £200.

Piccolo

Metal or wood. Length : 12½ in. approx.

The piccolo is the smallest instrument in the whole orchestra, yet its tone is the brightest, and on occasions its voice can be heard above the sound of the full orchestra. The piccolo looks just like a half-sized flute. Most piccolos are made in two parts, (a head joint and body). Some, however, have a foot joint which gives the instrument an extra note.

A piccolo

15

Wood-wind Instruments

A fife and drum band

The piccolo sounds one octave (8 notes) higher than the flute, but its tone is more piercing and less full. It is a very difficult instrument to learn to play.

Tchaikovsky wrote particularly well for the piccolo and his ballet music gives many excellent examples of its use.

The cost of a piccolo ranges from £40 to £75.

Alto Flute

This member of the flute family is sometimes called a bass flute. It is larger than the flute and sounds a fourth lower (i.e. four notes lower). It is rarely used nowadays, although several modern composers, such as Stravinsky and Britten, have written for it. The lower notes of its compass are unusually beautiful and have a strange, haunting quality.

Fife

The fife is between the flute and piccolo in range and has a very bright tone. It is the main instrument in the fife and drum band.

Recorder

Wood or plastic. Length: 9½ in. approx.

The recorder or long-blown flute will be familiar to most boys and girls. Nearly all schools have their own recorder groups and many young children begin their musical education with the recorder. Although it is possible to play tunes after a few lessons, boys and girls who play the recorder will know that to play it really well takes a great deal of time and practice.

16

There are five sizes of recorder : soprano, descant, treble, tenor and bass, and their length ranges from $9\frac{1}{2}$ inches to 38 inches. The compass of each instrument is :

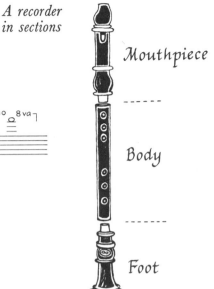

A recorder in sections

Mouthpiece

Body

Foot

Apart from solo use, recorders of different sizes go well together to form recorder bands. In the sixteenth and seventeenth centuries, recorders as well as viols played in consort, that is, in groups. Many references are made to the recorder in the writings of Shakespeare, Milton and Pepys. Henry VIII not only played the recorder but possessed over seventy of them. The recorder was a member of the orchestra in Bach's and Handel's time and both of these composers wrote a great deal of music for it.

The smaller recorders are usually made in two pieces : mouthpiece

A group of recorders : from left to right, a bass recorder, two tenor recorders, two treble recorders and three descant recorders

Wood-wind Instruments

A long-blown flute and a cross-blown flute played by Mr. Pepys and a friend

and body. The larger models are mostly made in three pieces : mouthpiece, body and foot. No key-work is used on these instruments and the eight holes are covered by the three middle fingers of each hand, the left thumb (the thumb hole is underneath) and the little finger of the right hand for the lowest note. On some modern instruments a key is provided for the lowest note.

The cross-blown flute player has to direct his breath against the edge of the mouth-hole in his instrument. The recorder player is more fortunate as he needs only to blow through the small hole in the mouthpiece and his breath is directed by the hole against the sharp edge of the sound-hole. The method of sound production and the way in which the instrument is held are the main differences between members of the flute and recorder families.

The recorders sound a rather gentle, hollow tone, which was ideal for the music of the sixteenth and seventeenth centuries. But as the orchestra grew in size, the recorder's place was taken by the cross-blown flute which has a much fuller tone. Before the seventeenth century, composers had used both types of flute, and when they wished the cross-blown flute to be used they marked the score *traversa* or *flauto traverso*.

In recent years, the Dolmetsch family have been largely responsible for the revival of the recorder and several modern composers have been so enchanted by its sound that they have composed music especially for it. The suites by Peter Crossley-Holland are excellent examples of modern recorder music.

Folk dancers accompanied by a flageolet

Flageolet

Another member of the recorder group is the flageolet. It differs from the recorder in detail only, two holes being placed underneath for the thumbs. It is rarely heard nowadays, and then only in folk music.

Tabor-Pipe

The pipe and tabor (see *tabor* in the percussion section) have from the Middle Ages been used for the accompaniment of folk dancing. As the picture shows, the pipe is played by the fingers of the left hand. There are three note-holes, two on top for the fingers and one underneath for the thumb. It has a compass of about one and a half octaves.

Tabor and pipe

19

Wood-wind Instruments

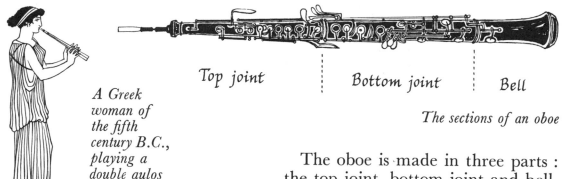

Top joint Bottom joint Bell

The sections of an oboe

A Greek woman of the fifth century B.C., playing a double aulos

Oboe

African blackwood, cocus and rosewood. Length : 1 ft. 11½ in.

The oboe began its life in about the year 1650, but its ancestry goes back many years earlier. The Greek aulos was an oboe-like instrument fitted with a double reed ; it was usually played in pairs.

Early oboes lacked key-work, having perhaps only one or two keys, the fingers covering the other holes. Over the years many improvements have been made and a system of key-work added.

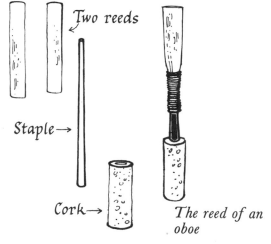

Two reeds

Staple →

Cork →

The reed of an oboe

The oboe is made in three parts : the top joint, bottom joint and bell. You will notice that the tube gradually widens into a bell-like shape at the bottom which gives the bell section its name.

The reed is also made in three parts : a cork base, staple and two pieces of reed cane. When assembled, it is pushed into the socket of the top joint, being held firmly in position by the cork base. The tip of the reed is placed on the lower lip with the upper lip closing over it. Both lips are then drawn or curled back over the teeth forming two cushions with the reed in between. When the lips are tightly closed and the breath forced between the reeds, the reeds vibrate and cause the air inside the oboe to vibrate and sound a note. The reed, if detached and blown through, makes a sound on its own which is called the *crow of the reed*.

Of the four primary wood-wind instruments (flute, oboe, clarinet, bassoon), the oboe has the smallest range, but no other wind instrument compares with it for vividness of colour, expressiveness and intensity of tone. It is an instrument which has its own special character, and it is often used for solo work, especially in pastoral music, that is, when the composer wishes us to feel the pleasure of being in the country.

The lower notes are full and heavy and difficult to play softly; the upper notes are thin and piercing. The oboe blends well with the strings and trumpets, giving an edge to the tone. Many other " blendings ", or to use the correct expression, *doublings*, are possible. Brahms, for example, doubles the horn with the oboe in

An oboe player

the slow movement of his Third Symphony.

The cost of an oboe varies from £50 to £200.

A cor anglais

Crook of cor anglais

Bach (1685–1750)

Cor Anglais

African blackwood. Length : 2ft. 7½ in.

This instrument sounds a fifth (i.e. five notes) lower than the oboe. If you compare it with the oboe, you will notice that the bell is larger and shaped differently, and the reed is placed on a metal crook, which is bent at an angle for the convenience of the player. The tone of the cor anglais is very beautiful and melancholy and most useful for solo passages. The majority of oboe players play the cor anglais. Bach used two

Wood-wind Instruments

instruments of this kind in his " St. Matthew Passion " with great effect, and in modern times Sibelius has written a most beautiful melody for it in " The Swan of Tuonela " which shows off the instrument to perfection.

Oboe d'amore

African blackwood or other special woods. Length : $25\frac{1}{2}$ in.

The oboe d'amore, like the cor anglais, is a lower version of the oboe. It sounds a minor third lower than the oboe and has a very sweet tone, perhaps a little softer than that of the oboe. Like the cor anglais, it has a pear-shaped bell. Today it can often be heard in the Passion and Christmas music of Bach.

The bass oboe and heckelphone are bass instruments of the oboe family and both produce a rich and heavy tone. Both instruments are larger than the cor anglais, but otherwise resemble it in shape. They are rarely heard, though Delius,

From a mediaeval manuscript. The musicians are playing a lute, a shawm and a harp.

Sibelius (1865–1957)

Strauss and Holst wrote works using them.

Shawm

This instrument was one of the oboe's predecessors and had a very fierce, penetrating tone, which was best used in combination with trumpets.

By the beginning of the eighteenth century it had become almost extinct, and the only place in Europe where it lives on is in the north of Spain and just north of the Pyrenees in France. There it can still be heard in the bands that play for the ancient dances.

Clarinet

African blackwood, ebonite. Length : $26\frac{1}{2}$ in. B flat clarinet. $27\frac{3}{4}$ in. A clarinet.

Nuremberg is the birthplace of the clarinet. It was made by a man

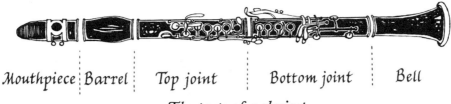

The parts of a clarinet

Mouthpiece | Barrel | Top joint | Bottom joint | Bell

named Denner in 1690. Its ancestors can be traced back to the ancient Arabian instrument called a *zummara*. This instrument can be seen on some ancient Egyptian tablets dating back to 3000 B.C.

The modern clarinet is made in five parts : bell, bottom joint, top joint, mouthpiece and barrel. The mouthpiece is usually made of ebonite, although other materials have been used, including plastics.

One reed is required—it is longer and wider than the oboe reed and is clamped to the mouthpiece by the *ligature*. The clarinet is a *single reed instrument*.

The embouchure is not quite so difficult as that of the oboe. It is formed by the player putting about half an inch of the mouthpiece, reed downwards, between the lips. The lower lip is curled back to form a cushion between the reed and teeth. The top teeth are placed directly on the mouthpiece, or, if the player prefers, the top lip can cushion the teeth. The lips are then puckered

tightly round the reed to prevent the air escaping ; the breath sets the reed in vibration.

As with other instruments, the early models had little or no key-work. The Boehm system of key-work is the most commonly used nowadays.

The clarinet possesses the largest range of the wood-wind instruments. Its three *registers*, bottom, middle and top are quite distinctive. The bottom register is also known as the *chalumeau* register, after an obsolete instrument of the same family played at the time of the clarinet's invention. This low register has a full,

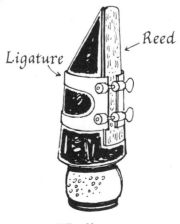

The ligature

Wood-wind Instruments

A bass clarinet

rich and smooth sound ; the middle register is clear and bell-like ; and the top register is piercing and rather harsh.

Bass Clarinet

This instrument began its life about the year 1838. It possesses a smooth, rich tone and has been used with great effect by Wagner, Puccini and Delius.

Nowadays it can be seen and heard in the majority of concerts given by our big symphony orchestras.

Basset Horn

The basset horn was invented about the year 1770 and its tone is a little rougher than that of the clarinet. Mozart and Strauss used it a great deal. As very few instruments exist today, their parts are given to other clarinets.

A basset horn

Bassoon

European maple.
Length of tube : 8 ft.

As with the other wood-wind instruments, the ancestors of the bassoon can be traced back to ancient times. The primitive treble bombard (shawm) evolved into the oboe family, and the bass bombard into the bassoon family, about the year 1600.

The bassoon has five parts : the crook (of metal), tenor joint, butt, long joint, and the bell. The double reed, which has a different shape from that of the oboe reed, is fitted directly on to the end of the crook.

Being a long instrument, it is doubled back on itself for obvious reasons, and is supported by a special sling which is placed round the neck. It has an embouchure similar to that of the oboe and a system of key-work and holes specially constructed owing to the length of the instrument.

There are 17 keys on the modern bassoon. The most sought-after instruments are made by the German firm of Heckel. A new instrument suitable for a beginner costs about £125.

Apart from its important place as the bass instrument of the wood-wind group, it has a life of its own as a solo instrument. Quick passages and tunes which skip about with large intervals between the notes are in keeping with the character of the bassoon. The tone of the bassoon is quite distinctive ; it is powerful and penetrating in the low register and rather hollow in the top register. The sound of its top register can best be described as a mixture of male voice and horn.

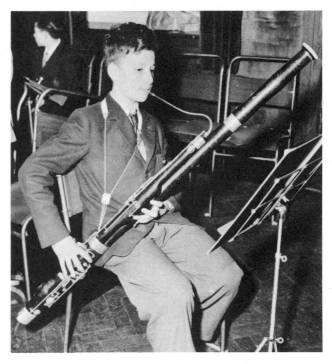

A bassoon player

It blends well with the string and brass groups and blends so well with the horns that it is often used as an extra horn.

Double or Contra Bassoon

8va bassa

European maple. Length of tube : 16 ft.

The double bassoon sounds one octave lower than the bassoon and produces a smooth, velvety tone. It is used in most of our symphony orchestras, and can easily be recognised because of its size. The deepest notes in the wood-wind section of the orchestra are played by the double

A bombard player of the fifteenth century

Wood-wind Instruments

A double bassoon

bassoon, and its tone blends well with the lower strings.

Saxophones

The saxophone group of instruments was invented by Adolphe Sax in 1840. These instruments use a single reed like a clarinet and are made of metal.

Generally, saxophones produce a tight tone which is full and rich in quality. They are used chiefly but not by any means only in the dance band. Many of our famous composers, Vaughan Williams and William Walton to mention just two, have used them in their orchestral works. They blend well with the strings and can play very softly. The complete family consists of a sopranino, soprano, alto, tenor, baritone, bass and contra-bass. Of these the alto, tenor and baritone are the only members in general use.

Jazz and dance bands very often use a group of four or five saxophones as the sweetness of their tone and the ease with which they can play rapid passages make them particularly suitable for this kind of music.

The wood-wind section of a large dance orchestra

3. The Brass Group

In 1800, when Beethoven was thirty years old, the brass section of an orchestra was smaller than it is today. At that time the composer used 2 horns and 2 trumpets, with an extra horn or two and trombones for special effects. Today, in a symphony orchestra, there are 4 horns, 3 trumpets, 3 trombones and a tuba. Extra horns and trumpets are often added.

Brass, or some other metal or alloy, is used to make the instruments. Their sound is made, as with the wood-wind instruments, by making the air inside vibrate. The embouchure of the brass instruments is different from that of the wood-wind

The player of a brass instrument uses his lips as reeds

group, for the player uses his own lips as reeds. He places his lips, almost closed, against the cup-shaped mouthpiece and makes them vibrate when he forces his breath between them. In turn, the air-stream from the player's lips vibrates and, passing through the neck of the mouthpiece, causes the air inside the tube to vibrate.

It is possible to obtain from *any* tube a series of about 16 notes. This is because of the natural law which enables the player to sound the notes by altering the speed of the vibration of the air in the tube. These notes are obtained by altering the pressure of the lips; the tighter the lips the greater the compression (which means that the air is more tightly

*Beethoven
(1770–1827)*

27

Brass Group

The series of 16 notes for a tube sounding C as its lowest or fundamental note.

pressed together) and the more rapid the vibration of the air-stream. The more rapid the vibration, the higher the note. The looser the lips, the slower the vibration and the lower the note.

You may wonder why the wood-wind and brass each use a different way of making their notes. This is because the ease with which notes can be made from a tube by altering the lip pressure depends on the length of the tube and the width of the bore (this is the name of the hole that is bored inside the tube). With the wood-wind instruments, the length of the tube and the width of the bore is too small for the notes to be made by lip pressure, as too much would be required and no player could press his lips together tightly enough to make the notes.

Brass instruments which have longer tubes and wider bores, require less lip pressure, therefore the player's lips are used to make the air vibrate.

The main difference between the wood-wind and brass instruments is the way in which they are played, and not the material from which they are made.

Two bassoons (woodwind) and four trumpets (brass) in the National Youth Orchestra

An ivory horn known as an oliphant

Horn

ORCHESTRAL HORN

Brass. Length of the tube of the orchestral horn : over 11 ft.

The horn was originally the horn of an animal—and the name and shape, wide at one end and narrowing to almost a point at the other, have remained much the same throughout the centuries. A bronze horn was used for hunting and signalling during the Middle Ages and an ivory horn, known as an oliphant, was carried by a knight as a token of his rank.

As the instrument " grew up " it also grew longer so that more notes could be played. To make it easy to carry it was curled in large loops so that it would fit round the body.

It was this version of the horn that first found its way into the orchestra in about the year 1700. Having so few notes, especially in the lower part of its compass, it could only be given very simple tunes or rhythmical patterns to play. That is why in some symphonies written in the early eighteenth century you will often hear passages like this,

From the last movement of Symphony No. 39 by Mozart.

which has more rhythm than tune. Sometimes, however, you will hear a tune using the high notes of the horn. This is because there are more notes available in the top register of the horn for writing tunes. The high notes require great skill to play well, as they need very firm lip pressure.

An eighteenth-century huntsman

29

Brass Group

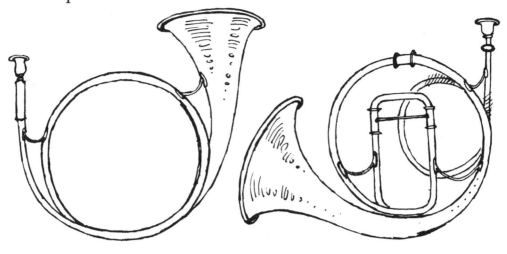

A natural horn and a natural horn with crooks

To play with tight lips (for the high notes), or loose lips (for the low notes), requires a great deal of practice and not many players can do both well. In modern orchestras, where 4 horns are used, the first and third players specialise in playing the high notes, the second and fourth players in playing the low notes.

When the horn became an orchestral instrument, a device known as a *crook* was invented. This was a short length of tubing made to slot into the horn tube ; in fact, several different lengths of crook were used.

The effect of adding a crook was to make the horn tube longer. By changing the crooks it was possible to pitch the series of notes in a number of different scales. If you look at the score of an eighteenth-century orchestral work, perhaps by Haydn or Mozart, you will notice that horns in G, F, E flat, or some other key, are required. This means that the composer wishes the horns to pitch their series of notes in, for example, the key of F, and the players will need to use the F crook.

Some of the notes produced by the natural horn sound out of tune, but by putting his right hand into the bell of the instrument the player can alter the pitch of the notes to make them in tune. These are called *stopped notes.*

The valve horn is the instrument that is used in the modern orchestra. The player, instead of changing the crooks from time to time, presses the valve keys. This brings into use the crooks, and the player, by moving his fingers, can pitch the series of notes in many keys. All these extra notes now enable him to make a complete scale over the compass of his instrument.

The tube of the horn is shaped like a long-drawn-out cone, curled round and round, opening out into a bell at one end : on the other end is fitted a special funnel-shaped mouthpiece.

A valve horn

Today, the horn is often called the French horn. This is probably because in France where the details of the hunt were highly organised and many horn calls and signals were used, the horn developed more quickly as an instrument.

The horn can be played very softly and expressively, and the sound can

be made to die away almost to nothing. On the other hand, it can be played loudly with great brilliance. The high notes are very penetrating and stand out above the full orchestra—these are difficult to play softly. The middle and low notes can be played softly or loudly and have a velvet quality of sound. Besides slow tunes, composers also give the horn bright march-like tunes to play and passages of notes repeated very rapidly.

Sometimes at concerts you will notice a player putting a cone into the bell of the horn. This is called a *mute* and it makes the horn sound far away. If the player uses a mute and blows with force, the sound is harsh and catches the attention at once.

The horn is a very difficult instrument to learn to play.

Horns in the orchestra

Brass Group

Trumpet

Brass or metal alloy. Length of tube : about 4½ ft.

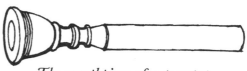

The mouthpiece of a trumpet

In many ways the trumpet is similar to the horn in development and construction. The first trumpets were natural trumpets, which were followed by natural trumpets with crooks and then by valve trumpets. The trumpet plays higher notes than the horn and the tone is much brighter. The main differences between the two instruments are in the length of the tube, the shape of the bore (which in the trumpet is of even width

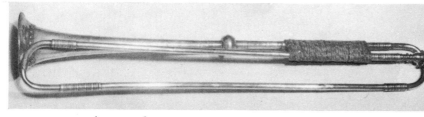

A natural trumpet

for most of its length), the size of the bell and the mouthpiece (the mouthpiece of the trumpet is cup-shaped).

In Bach's time, when crooks were used less frequently than at a later period, trumpet players used instruments pitched in different keys instead of changing the pitch by means of a crook. Orchestral trumpet players of those days would have three or four trumpets by their side and change them as required. Bach wrote tunes for his trumpets using the high notes, which are very difficult to play.

The natural trumpet with crooks began to be used in the orchestra about the year 1700. Using only the natural series of notes, its use in the orchestra was limited to rhythmical, fanfare-like passages and simple tunes. However, Bach and his fellow composers sometimes used the brilliant top notes for a more melodic part. Haydn and Mozart did not use the high notes very often ; even Beethoven, with all his ideas and powerful music, did not write melodic parts for the trumpet.

About 1885 a straight trumpet, with valves and a special mouthpiece, was made to play the top notes, and was known as the Bach trumpet. Nowadays a folded or curled instrument with valves pitched in D, is used.

A straight trumpet

A valve trumpet

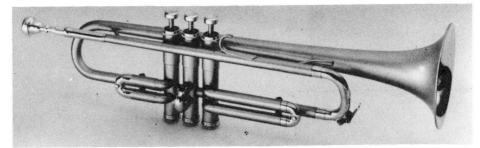

It was not until the end of the nineteenth century that the modern valve trumpet came into being. Its sound is noble, brilliant and very commanding. The tone is bright and ringing and can be heard through the full orchestra.

For centuries, the trumpet has sounded in times of triumph and disaster; it has long been the friend of kings and soldiers and its voice has been heard at many a dramatic moment in history. It was heard at the Coronation Banquet of King Henry VIII: " At the bryngyng of the first course the trumpettes blew up and in came the Duke of Buckyngham mounted upon a great courser, richly trapped and embroidered ".

Sentimental tunes are not typical of the instrument, though the trumpet can be muted to sound distant when played softly, and rather rasping when played with more force.

It is a difficult, but thrilling instrument to learn to play.

A group of heralds in ceremonial dress playing trumpets

Brass Group

A sackbut

Trombone

BASS TROMBONE

TENOR TROMBONE

Also possible

Brass or metal alloy. Length of tube :
12 ft. $\frac{1}{4}$ in. Bass Trombone
8 ft. 10 in. Tenor Trombone

The trombone, called by its old name of sackbut, is often mentioned in ancient writings. It may date back to Roman times, but there is some doubt about this. We do know, however, that as early as the beginning of the fourteenth century the sackbut looked almost exactly like our modern trombone. In 1495 Henry VII had four " shakbusshes " in his court, and Henry VIII had ten.

The trombone has been referred to as a double trumpet. This is one of the best ways to describe it, for it has the same nobility and brilliance of tone as the trumpet, especially in the top part of its voice, and is twice its size. The lower notes are particularly beautiful when played softly ; they sound round and smooth, not unlike soft, deep horns. Muted, its sound can die away to almost a whisper. Instead of using crooks or valves to alter the length of the tube, a slide is used. This is pushed forward or backwards by the right hand.

Like the other brass instruments, the trombone uses the natural series of notes. By altering the position of the slide, (there are seven positions), different series of notes are obtained to make up a complete scale throughout the range of the instru-

A trombone

ment. It has the same kind of bore and mouthpiece as the trumpet, and a medium-sized bell.

In a full symphony orchestra, 3 trombones are used, 2 tenor trombones and 1 bass trombone. When loud, they sound majestic ; and when soft, magical and full of mystery.

Tuba

Brass or metal alloy. Length of tube : 16 ft.

Many boys and girls may have already made a friend of the tuba through a popular song called " Tubby the Tuba ". In many ways this is a good description of the instrument, for it is rather " tubby " and its tone, too, is very smooth and round.

A tuba

Vaughan Williams (1872–1958)

In 1845, five years after the appearance of the saxophone, Adolphe Sax produced another group of instruments which he called saxhorns. The tuba is the bass instrument of this group and is called a bass saxhorn. It is not looked upon as a solo instrument and is rarely heard on its own, although Vaughan Williams wrote a concerto for it.

Its sound is produced by using the natural series of notes, and valves ; the mouthpiece is cup-shaped.

Brass and military bands use tubas, but they are called by different names : euphonium, bombardon and baritone. They differ only slightly from the tuba in construction and tone.

The number of keys or valves used by the instruments of the tuba family varies from three to five.

35

Brass Group

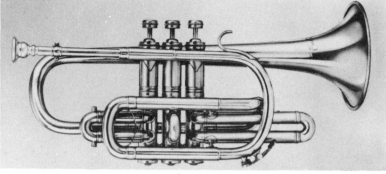

A cornet

Cornet or Cornet-a-Piston

Brass or metal alloy. Length of tube : 4 ft. 5 in. to 4 ft. 8 in.

The cornet developed out of a simple horn-like instrument used in France about 1827. It has three valves which operate in the same way as trumpet valves, and in appearance it is not unlike the trumpet. Its tone is halfway between that of the trumpet and horn, but having a wider bore than either, the production of the notes is easier. It blends well with the trumpet and horn, but lacks the brilliance of the one and the mellowness of the other. Perhaps, for this reason, it is not very often used in our symphony orchestras. Certain compositions require the use of trumpets as well as cornets, for example the Symphony in D Minor by César Franck. The ease with which cornets can be played makes them most suitable for use in military and brass bands, and in orchestras that play light music.

Bugle

Brass or copper.

The main use of the bugle is for military calls. It is related to the trumpet and horn by its shape and the way it is played. Most bugles are made without keys or pistons and can produce only a few notes.

Their tone is very piercing and is ideal for use in the open air.

A bugler of the French Army in the time of Napoleon

36

4. Stringed Instruments

Stringed instruments can be divided into two main groups, those that are played with a bow, and those that are played by plucking the strings. Later you will read about another group of stringed instruments which are played by means of a keyboard.

Bowed Instruments

When we talk about the *strings* of the orchestra we are referring to the violin family of instruments. The four instruments of this group—namely, the violin, viola, violoncello and double bass—have many points in common. Their main difference is one of size. As a

The string family : double bass, violin, viola and 'cello

Stringed Instruments

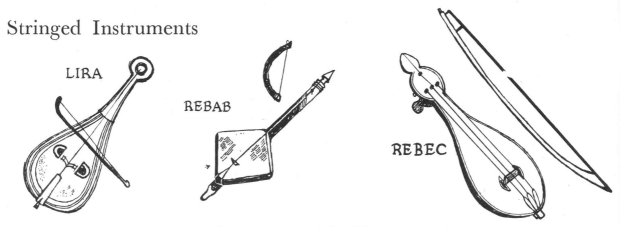

Some ancestors of the violin

family, their shape and sound has altered very little from the time they emerged (about 1600), to the present day.

Sometimes all the instruments of this family were called by the name of "violin"; Louis XIV had a complete string band attached to his Court, and referred to it as a "band of twenty-four violins".

The violin family grew out of different stringed instruments of earlier centuries. In the ninth century there was an instrument called a fiddle, and from Byzantium in the eleventh century the lira came to Europe. An ancestor in the twelfth century was called a guitar-fiddle and another in the thirteenth century the rebec, which came from the Arabian rebab.

The Bow

Throughout the centuries, the shape of the bow has changed a great deal, and the bow used today grew into its present shape about the end of the eighteenth century. Even to-day, the viol bow (see page 46) is used by some players when performing music written before the new bow came into use. The modern bow is made of a strong flexible stick (rosewood, pernambuco wood, snake wood) and about 200 hairs from the tail of a horse.

By means of a screw at the heel of the bow, the hairs can be made tight

A guitar-fiddle and bow of the twelfth century

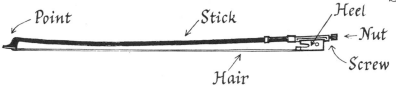

A modern bow

or loose. Under a microscope, small ends can be seen sticking out rather like thorns on a briar. With the help of a substance called resin, which is rubbed over the hairs, these " thorns " grip the strings of the violin as the bow is drawn across, causing them to vibrate.

Besides making the strings sing lovely melodies, the bow can be made to bounce on the strings to produce short, dancing notes.

The tone, too, can be varied by the bow. This is done by altering the speed at which it moves over the strings, the pressure, and the position on the strings (i.e., near the finger-board, near the bridge or mid-way between).

Making a bow is a skilled craft and a good bow may cost as much as £50.

The normal way of playing the instruments of the violin family is by means of the bow. But you will probably have noticed that the strings can also be plucked with the tip of a finger. This is called *pizzicato*, which is an Italian word meaning " plucked ". When all the strings of an orchestra play pizzicato, they sound rather like a big harp, although the sound is shorter and " drier ".

Composers mark their scores *pizzicato* when they want the notes to be plucked. When they want the bow to be used they use the word *arco*. This Italian word means " bow ". Another effect, which sounds like the rattle of dry sticks, is obtained by tapping the strings with the wooden back of the bow. This is called, again, by an Italian word, *legno*, which means " wood ".

A violin player in a school orchestra

Stringed Instruments

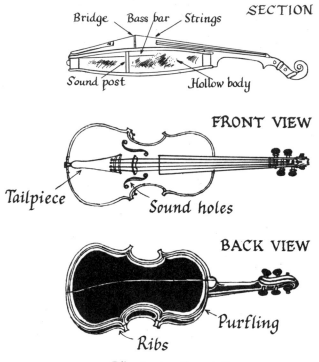

SECTION

Bridge   Bass bar   Strings

Sound post   Hollow body

FRONT VIEW

Tailpiece   Sound holes

BACK VIEW

Purfling

Ribs

The parts of a violin

The pictures on these two pages show the parts of the instruments belonging to the violin group. Look at them carefully as they will be referred to during this chapter.

When the strings are set in vibration by the bow or fingers, the sound waves travel through the bridge and sound-post into the hollow body of the instrument. By a scientific process, the body makes the sound waves more beautiful and louder, and they flow out of the body through the sound holes.

The four strings are tuned a fifth apart, except those of the double bass which are tuned a fourth apart. This is done by turning the pegs to tighten the strings. The greater the tension, or tightness, the higher the note. You can find this out for yourselves by plucking a piece of tightly stretched elastic. When you stretch it even tighter the pitch of the note is altered. This is what happens when violin strings are tuned. The tension on some of the strings is equal to the pull of a 90 lb. weight.

When the strings have been tuned, the pitch of any one string can be raised by pressing the string against the fingerboard with a finger of the left hand.

This is because the effect of pressing the string against the fingerboard is the same as shortening the string. Players sometimes press the strings very lightly. This causes the strings to make faint notes at a higher pitch, giving an effect called *harmonics*.

The work of stopping the strings with the left hand and of controlling the movement of the bow with the right is very difficult and both actions have to be done together.

Most of the strings are made from twisted strips of specially prepared sheep-gut. Nowadays nylon and metal strings are widely used as they are stronger, although the tone is perhaps a little harder than from gut strings. By putting a mute on the bridge of a stringed instrument the tone can be changed and made to sound softer.

Sycamore, pine, ebony and rose-wood are all used to make different parts of the stringed instruments. The body and neck are covered with many coats of varnish to preserve the wood and to improve the tone.

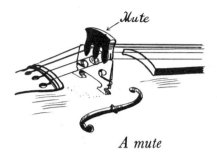

A mute

Violin

Most boys and girls will know what a violin sounds and looks like ; it is perhaps the most familiar of all the orchestral instruments.

Each of its four strings, G, D, A and E has its own tone-colour. The E string is nearly always made of metal and has a much brighter and harder sound than the gut strings. A wire string is used because the tension on this string is so great. Metal takes the strain much better and is less likely to break than gut.

There is no difference between the first and second violins in the orchestra, except in the parts that they are given to play.

The most sought-after violins were made by Italian craftsmen of the seventeenth and eighteenth centuries. The most famous makers were Amati, Guarneri and Stradivari, all of whom lived in Cremona in Northern Italy. Instruments by these early makers can nowadays cost many thousands of pounds. If you want to learn to play the violin, a good instrument can be bought for as little as £10.

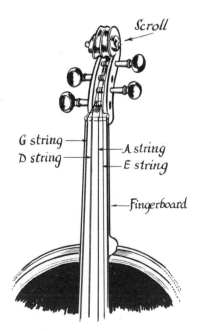

The fingerboard and scroll of a violin

Stringed Instruments

Viola

The viola has been the Cinderella of the violin group. This is probably because it is so tiring to play, being larger and heavier than the violin, and the parts written for it are not always so interesting to play as those written for the violin and 'cello.

The player must also learn to

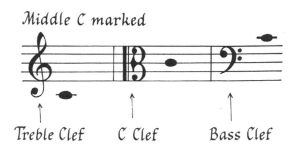

Middle C marked

Treble Clef   C Clef   Bass Clef

A clef is the sign placed at the beginning of the stave from which the name and position of the notes are found.

play from music written in another clef, the C clef, instead of the more usual treble and bass clefs, and his hand must be large, as the notes are further apart and need a wider stretch to play them.

Sir William Walton

The sound is full and rich, and the top notes have a very individual quality that is penetrating. In the orchestra it plays the middle notes, those between the notes of the violin and the 'cello. Fortunately, many famous composers such as Mozart and Bach, and in our time Sir William Walton, have been aware of its beauties and have written works for the viola.

'Cello

(Higher notes are possible, but not often used)

Although we use the name 'cello for this instrument, its correct name is violoncello. It is held between the knees (like the viola da gamba you

A 'cello

will be reading about later), and is supported by a steel spike which is pushed back into the belly of the instrument for carrying—early instruments were made without this spike.

Mozart (1756–1791)

The 'cello plays the lowest notes in a string quartet and most of the low notes in the orchestra. The tone is full and rich and so beautiful that composers often write tunes for the 'cello, besides giving it the bass or bottom part to play, which supports tunes played by other instruments. You could think of it as a violin with a deep voice. Many works have been written for the 'cello from Bach's time to the present day.

A double bass

Double Bass   *Sounding an octave lower*

This is the largest of all the orchestral instruments and plays the lowest notes in the orchestra. Being so large, the player has either to stand or sit on a stool. The shape and the size of the double bass have always varied ; some instruments have the sloping shoulders of the viol family and others are shaped like the violin. Early instruments only had 3 strings ; today, 4 strings are used, and occasionally 5. Unlike the other members of the violin family,

Stringed Instruments

it is tuned in fourths. This method of tuning avoids long stretches for the fingers. Like the tuba, it is rarely used as a solo instrument, although a few concertos have been written for it.

The notes of the double bass sound one octave lower than they are written, and in the orchestra they add depth and firmness to the music. On the other hand, they can give the music lightness and " spring " when they are played pizzicato. Not many boys and girls learn the bass because large hands are needed with fingers that can stretch wide apart, and of course the instrument itself is taller than many children. No orchestra is complete without its bass, and its job is very important. Like the tuba, basses rarely have tunes to play on their own, but when they join the 'cellos in a tune they add depth and richness.

The double bass is also used in dance bands where it is played pizzicato giving a steady rhythm to the music, which is essential for dancing.

Viols

In recent years another group of stringed instruments has come back into use, called the viols. Although there are three kinds, treble, tenor and bass, they are all usually referred to as viols. Sometimes the correct name of viola da gamba is used.

A bass viol made in 1701 (this viol is without the usual frets)

This Italian name means " leg-viol " and it is so called because it is held between the knees. As a family, these instruments were improved in Italy during the fifteenth century, and today they still have the same shape and 6 strings. In many homes in the fifteenth and sixteenth centuries it was quite usual to have a " chest " of viols (they were kept in a wooden chest), which consisted of six instruments, two of each size. As a matter of course they were played by several, if not all, members of a family.

44

A consort or group of viols in a seventeenth-century mansion

When concerts began to be performed in halls and other large buildings, some of the softer sounding instruments were replaced by others with a larger tone. This was the case with the viols. 16 treble viols playing the same part would not sound very loud or pleasant, but 16 violins playing together sound full and beautiful. From about 1600 the viol family began to be replaced by the violin family, although in this country the bass viol continued to be used for about another hundred years.

Musicians today try to give the music they play an accurate interpretation. This means the instruments used should be those that the composer wrote for ; this is one of the reasons why so many of the older, almost forgotten, instruments are coming back into use, including the viols.

Many people do not like the sound of the viol at first : it has a softer, more reedy and penetrating sound than that of the violin, with more edge to the tone.

Bach used the viola da gamba in his Sixth Brandenburg Concerto, and as a solo instrument with voice in his " St. John Passion " and " St. Matthew Passion ".

Stringed Instruments

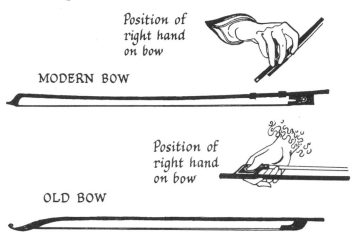

Position of
right hand
on bow

MODERN BOW

Position of
right hand
on bow

OLD BOW

The bow of a viol and of a violin

Listen, if you have the chance, to a viol, or consort of viols, as a group of viols is called. Their sound is full of charm and character, and much beautiful music has been written for them.

The bow used by the viols is different from the modern bow, as you will notice from the picture. The strongest part of the modern bow is at the heel, whereas in the old bow the strongest part is at the point.

Around the neck of the viols is tied a piece of gut at every half-note. This is called *fretting*. Other instruments, too, the guitar for example, are also fretted. Apart from marking the position of the notes the fretting also affects the sound. This is because the vibrating portion of the string is between the fret and the bridge, and not between the finger and the bridge, as the finger is placed behind the fret. The effect of the fret is to give the stopped notes (notes the strings sound when touched, or stopped, by the fingers) the same quality as the open notes.

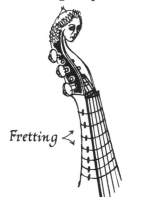

Fretting

Fretting on the fingerboard of a viol

Handel (1685–1759)

46

Other members of the viol family are the violone and the viola d'amore.

Violone

This is sometimes called a double bass viol or consort viol, and sounds an octave lower than the bass viol. Bach always wrote for this instrument in his cantatas. Today the part is played by the modern double bass which was derived from the violone.

Viola d'amore

Because of the soft, rich quality of its sound, this instrument has been called a " love viol ". Although it is usually grouped with the viols, it has several points in common with the violin family ; it is played like a violin and is without frets.

A viola d'amore

Vivaldi (1675–1741)

Unlike the viol, the viola d'amore has 14 strings. Of these, 7 are placed in the normal position over the finger-board and the other 7, made of wire, under the finger-board. The last 7 are called " sympathetic strings ". This is because they vibrate on their own in sympathy with the other strings, thus giving the instrument a tone unlike any other stringed instrument. Bach and Vivaldi wrote for the instrument, and Handel wrote for a smaller instrument of this kind, which of course played higher notes, called a violetta marina.

47

Stringed Instruments

An ancient Egyptian harp

pegs in the neck. The frame is made of wood and the strings of gut. The lowest eight strings are usually made of metal or silk and are over-spun with very fine wire.

The strings are tuned in the scale of C flat major and have a range of over six and a half octaves. Seven foot-pedals enable each string to be raised in pitch a half or a whole tone.

Plucked Instruments

This group of stringed instruments is played by plucking the strings with the fingers or with a plectrum, which is sometimes a quill or more usually a pear-shaped piece of tortoise shell.

Harp

Paintings of the harp have been found dating back to the thirteenth century B.C., and the remains of early examples have been found in the Egyptian tombs of a much earlier date.

The harp has a graceful shape and many are beautifully carved and decorated. The lower ends of the strings are fixed to a piece of wood which is glued to the centre of the sound board and the upper ends (of the strings) are attached to tuning-

A modern harp

48

The sound of the harp is not unlike the sound of the piano, but generally speaking that of the harp is rounder and more bell-like. The sweeping, swirling cascade of notes that is so often heard coming from the harp is called a *glissando* (derived from a French word " glisser " which means to slide) and is produced by drawing the fingers across the strings.

The harp first appeared in the orchestra in the early seventeenth century, in the small orchestras used for the performance of opera in Italy.

Handel, Gluck, Beethoven and Mozart rarely used the harp orchestrally, although Mozart wrote a concerto for it. Nowadays it is a regular member of our large symphony orchestras and many small bands of all kinds use a harp. Passages of glis-

A Gaelic harp. The twenty-nine brass strings were plucked with the player's finger-nails, grown long for the purpose.

sandos, *chords* (two or more notes played together) and *arpeggios* (the notes of a chord played one after the other), are most effective. It blends well with all the other instruments of the orchestra and is sometimes used to accompany a solo on one of the wood-wind instruments.

There are other kinds of harp such as the Welsh harp and Irish harp. These are smaller and are held in the hands. The troubadours and minnesingers of the eleventh century used a harp of this smaller kind to accompany their songs.

Lyre

This instrument was a small harp which was very popular with the Ancient Greeks, Assyrians and Hebrews. It differs from the normal harp in that the strings are stopped by the left hand ; a plectrum, held in the right hand, is used to sound the strings.

From a Greek vase (450 B.C.). The woman seated on the left is tuning a lyre

Stringed Instruments

A lute of the seventeenth century

Lute

The lute can be traced back to an ancient Oriental instrument whose body was made from a half gourd (a kind of fruit) covered with a stretched skin. In the seventeenth century it was very popular, and had by then acquired about 26 or more strings. A great deal of very beautiful music was composed for it, and Bach included it as a tone-colour in his orchestral " paintbox ".

The finger-board has raised frets (as with the viols) marking the position of each semi-tone, and the strings are duplicated in unison (or in the same pitch).

The sound of the lute is rather like that of a soft harp ; it is one of the gentlest sounds in music. No description of the sounds of old instruments such as the lute, can give any more than a very hazy idea of the beautiful sounds many of them make. If the occasion comes your way to hear one, either on the wireless or at a recital, make the most of the opportunity to listen. Many players of stringed instruments today are making a special study of the art of playing old instruments.

Back view of a lute

An Elizabethan gentleman entertains a friend on the cittern during a visit to the barber.

Cittern

This instrument was very popular in Shakespeare's time and was to be found in barbers' shops for the use of customers.

50

Archlute

This is the largest member of the family. It has a double set of tuning pegs, and some strings that are not over the finger-board, which can only be played as open strings. The theorbo is sometimes called an archlute, although it is generally smaller.

Mandoline

The mandoline is like the lute in shape and is played with a plectrum instead of the fingers. It has 8 strings tuned in pairs.

A mandoline from Italy. The strings were of catgut and wire.

An archlute made in Venice in 1608. It is 6 feet long.

A Spanish guitar of the sixteenth century

Guitar

Although this instrument is often played in a dance band, its first use is as a solo instrument. It is very old, and is particularly popular in Spain. It has 6 strings plucked by the fingers and possesses a beautiful, lute-like tone. Many great composers have written music for it. Vivaldi and Schubert did so, and the great violinist Paganini thought so highly of the instrument that he left the violin for three years

Stringed Instruments

Spanish dancers accompanied by a guitar and other stringed instruments

in order to study the guitar. Like many other instruments of the lute type, it has frets on the finger-board to mark the half-tones.

Banjo

The banjo is thought to be of African origin. A type of banjo was probably played by the negro slaves who were taken from Africa to America; and it was from these slaves that the "Black and White" Minstrel bands developed. The sound-box of the banjo is made of a metal hoop with parchment stretched over one end, the other being left open. Its tone is very dry and brittle and is best suited to music of a light and rhythmical nature.

A "Black and White" Minstrel band

5. Percussion

Percussion instruments used by the Ancient Egyptians : cymbals, bells, crotales (metal castanets) and a sistrum (a rattle threaded with metal discs)

Kettledrums and tambourines were used in the temple worship of the Sumerian people in Ancient Mesopotamia and the Ancient Egyptians used a variety of percussion instruments. All through the years, countless percussion instruments of many civilisations have been used in the affairs of man : worship, dancing, signalling, marching, battle and many other activities have all had their particular percussion instruments to play the special rhythms connected with these events.

The percussion instruments give composers a fascinating collection of sounds and tone-colours to use. Many of the instruments have no definite pitch, while others can be tuned. The sounds are produced by striking, either with a special stick or hammer, or, in the case of pairs of instruments such as the cymbals, by dashing them together.

Many people have the idea that percussion instruments are easy to play. Certainly some of them do not require great skill, but percussion players are expected to play many different instruments.

During an orchestral work, a percussion player may be required to play a few bars on the bass drum, quickly change to the cymbals, then play a triangle and end up by playing on the xylophone. It is common today for orchestras to have two players in the percussion section, one for the kettle-drums, which are the most frequently used, and one for the other instruments. In some works requiring many percussion instruments, as many as four players will be needed.

In a dance band the percussion player is responsible (with the double bass) for giving a rhythmical background which is a very important

Percussion

part of this kind of music. Because of its job in a dance band the percussion section is often called the rhythm section.

Kettledrum or Tympani

These are the only drums which can sound notes of a definite pitch. Because of this they are very useful in the orchestra and blend in well with the other instruments. It is quite usual for two tympani to be the only percussion instruments used in a concert. They are mostly tuned to the " doh " and " soh ", or, to put it another way, the first and fifth notes of the scale in which the music is written.

On the top of the metal shell, which is shaped like a basin or half

Kettledrums

an egg, is placed a wooden hoop, over which a skin is stretched. This is held in position by a metal ring which is fixed on the shell. By means of the screws placed around the top of the drum the tension of the skin can be changed. The tighter the skin is drawn the higher is the pitch of the note.

The range or compass of a pair of kettledrums is small ; any two notes between

can be selected. You will often notice at a concert a player with his ear close to the drum, tapping it gently with his finger or stick. This is because the composer wants a different tuning and the player is re-tuning his drum. A few bars' rest is sufficient time for the player to turn the screws for the other notes.

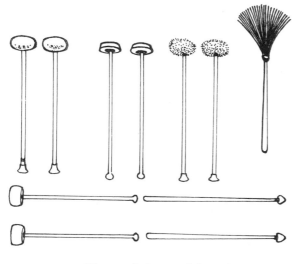

Types of drum stick

54

Nowadays drums are made with a special foot pedal for an almost immediate change of pitch and this type is becoming more frequently used.

A variety of drum sticks is used, each making a different sound. The sticks are made of cane ; some have padded ends, others a specially shaped wooden head. Sometimes a stick with a wire brush at the end is used.

The Crusaders may have brought the kettledrums to Europe from the East where drums were sometimes carried on each side of camels. From the Crusades until the sixteenth century, kettledrums were known as " nakeres " or " nakers " ; Chaucer calls them by this name in " The Canterbury Tales ". They must still have been rare for, as late as 1542,

Military kettledrums of Marlborough's time

Henry VIII sent to Vienna for drums that could be played on horseback " after the Hungarian manner ". By the seventeenth century, kettledrums were played by cavalry drummers in European armies when a pair of drums was slung on each side of a horse in front of the saddle.

Orchestrally, kettledrums were first used in Europe in 1675 by Lully, a French composer. In England, a composer called Locke used them a little earlier, and by the time of Purcell's opera, " The Fairy Queen " (1692), they were firmly established.

Purcell (1659–1695)

Percussion

Side Drum

This is a small cylindrical drum, with vellum or plastic stretched over each end. On the lower end *snares* are fixed (strings stretched across and touching the vellum); these give a rattling sound when the drum is struck. On some drums, a lever lifts the snares clear of the vellum if the rattling effect is not required.

The player uses two wooden drum sticks to produce the sound. In military bands the drum is slung to the player's side, and because of this it is called a side drum.

Its quiet tap in rhythmical music and its roll (loud and soft) are often heard in the orchestra. Sometimes a conductor begins the National

A side drum

Anthem with a side drum roll, starting softly and getting louder quickly. Another sound is produced by muffling the drum. This is done by means of a special lever which stops the effect of the snares.

A military bandsman with his side drum slung in position

Tenor Drum

This drum is also slung to the player's side, and in size is between the bass drum and side drum. The chief difference between the side drum and tenor drum, apart from size, is that the tenor drum is without snares. It is not used so frequently as the side and bass drums.

When the tenor and side drums are used in the orchestra the player fixes them to a special metal stand instead of slinging them to his side.

Bass Drum

This is the largest drum used and is without snares. It has a narrow cylindrical shell made of wood and is covered at both ends with stretched vellum. Another type of bass drum that is sometimes used has a cylindrical shell larger in diameter, which is covered at one end only. Both drums are struck with a stick with a large padded end. When played loudly these bass drums can sound like thunder and when softly, like a very distant deep explosion. Both are awe-inspiring sounds, and are most useful for the composer.

A bass drum in the percussion section of the orchestra

Usually the bass drum is heard in military, brass and dance bands, but it is also used in the orchestra.

Tabor or Taboret

The tabor is usually played with the tabor-pipe (see tabor-pipe in wood-wind section). The fingers of the player's left hand are used for the pipe, and the tabor is hung under the left arm with the stick in the player's right hand. In Provence in France it is still used today. Very occasionally it is used in the orchestra.

Tambourine

The tambourine is almost the same today as it was in Roman times. It is a small wooden hoop covered on

Tabor and pipe

Percussion

one side with stretched vellum or parchment. In the side of the hoop are small pairs of metal discs called *jingles*. The tambourine can be played by striking it with the knuckles, by shaking it to produce a jingling sound, and by rubbing the end of a moistened thumb over the parchment which sets the jingles in motion.

It is often used in the orchestra, particularly to give to dance movements suitable colour and atmosphere and for rhythmical patterns. Dancers in the Middle Ages used the tambourine alone as a rhythmical accompaniment.

Part of a mosaic from Pompeii showing a Roman tambourine

Triangle

The name triangle is given to this instrument because of its shape. A

Tambourine

small metal beater is used to sound the triangle which is hung from either the player's hand or a music stand. If the beater is placed in the middle of the triangle and moved to and fro rapidly, the triangle rings like a bright bell. Single strokes cause the triangle to " ting " clearly. Gluck was the first composer to use the triangle in the orchestra in 1779. Today it is often heard in the orchestra, especially in music that is bright and gay.

Castanets

The home of the castanets is Spain where they are called *castanuelas*. They are made from two small, hollow, shell-shaped pieces of hard wood. These are attached to the finger and thumb of each hand and " clacked " together. Sometimes they are hinged together with a piece of string and looped over the thumb, the fingers clacking them together.

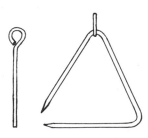

Triangle and beater

Castanets

For use in the orchestra they are fastened to a stick which is shaken as required. Their main use is in music that has the character of a Spanish dance. Bizet, a French composer, used them in his opera "C a r m e n", which is set in Spain.

The Spanish dancer, Antonio, with castanets

Cymbals

Cymbals are made from plates of brass with leather handles on the back. They are usually held in the two hands and clashed together, but sometimes one is fixed on to the side of a drum and the other clashed against it, or a single cymbal is suspended and struck with a tympani stick. A roll on a suspended cymbal is also possible by using 2 drum sticks. Players can produce another effect by rattling cymbals together at the edges. To make a short, sharp clash on the cymbals the player, after clashing them together, quickly pulls them against his body, which immediately stops the ringing sound ;

Cymbals

this is called "damping the cymbals".

When they are struck loudly, they make a shattering sound which can be heard over the full orchestra. Composers often save a cymbal crash until the music reaches the biggest climax of a movement, when it adds a final "blaze of light", which makes the climax the thrilling moment it should be. Another lovely effect can be made by playing a very quiet roll on a suspended cymbal with two soft tympani sticks ; this seems to add a thread of gold to the music. Berlioz, a French composer in the early 1800's, used the smaller type of cymbal, called ancient cymbals, which could be tuned to definite notes (unlike the other cymbals which have no definite pitch).

Cymbals of 2000 years ago

59

Percussion

Gong

The best gongs are made in the East and look like large plates made of metal with a turned-up rim. There are several sizes of gong, the deepest tones coming from the largest gongs. They are hung from a wood or metal frame and struck with a soft-headed stick. The sound a gong makes is rather like an enormous cymbal and is very awe-inspiring. For dramatic moments in music it is often used, soft or loud, with great effect.

A gong

Glockenspiel

Glockenspiel is a German name which means "bell-play". It is a set of steel plates played with two small hammers. The sound is bright and sparkling, rather like sunlight glinting on the sea. In the time of Mozart and Handel, real bells instead of steel plates were used.

Most of the instruments in use today are made with a little keyboard similar to that of the piano, and played in the same manner as the piano. The compass of the instrument is quite small, sounding one octave higher than the piano. Many composers use the glockenspiel today in all kinds of music, from dance music to symphonic music. It makes a delicate sound and adds colour and point to musical phrases.

A glockenspiel

A dulcimer: this instrument developed from the psaltery, which was played by plucking the strings with the fingers or a plectrum.

Dulcimer

Although some boys and girls will, perhaps, have had a dulcimer as a toy when they were very young, not many will know that it is an instrument that was in use in England about the year 1400. Pepys, the famous diarist, heard it at a puppet show in 1662, but after that date it seems to have dropped out of use.

It is a small shallow closed box on which are strung wires; these are struck with small wooden hammers.

In Eastern Europe, the instrument is still used. The players of the gypsy bands of Rumania and Hungary use a more elaborate dulci-mer than the earlier instrument and are brilliant players. The dulcimer is also known by its Hungarian name of *cymbalon*. The famous Hungarian composer, Kodaly, used the cymbalon in his orchestral suite, " Hary Janos ".

Celesta

The celesta was invented about 1880 by Mustel. It is a set of steel plates like the glockenspiel, but each plate is attached to a wooden resonator which gives the tone its very individual quality. The steel plates are struck by hammers which are operated from a small keyboard.

A celesta

61

Percussion

It is very difficult to describe its sound—it is soft, but clear and seems to float in the air. Tchaikovsky gives us an excellent opportunity to hear it in the " Dance of the Sugar Plum Fairy " from his " Nutcracker Suite ".

Tubular Bells

As the picture shows, these sets of bells are made from metal tubes which also give them their name. They are hung on a wooden frame and have a compass of about an octave and a half.

They are frequently used in the orchestras of today, especially for descriptive or joyful music, as in the church scene in Puccini's opera, " Tosca ".

Tubular bells

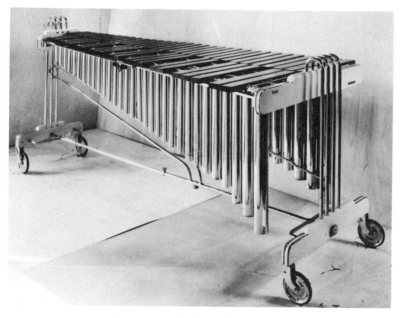

A xylophone

Xylophone

The xylophone is very much like the glockenspiel but it has bars of hard wood instead of bars of steel. It is played by means of two small mallets or beaters held in the hands. Some xylophones made today have metal tubes placed underneath the wooden bars, which act as resonators and make the tone less dry.

Saint-Saens, the French composer, has used the xylophone very effectively in his " Dance Macabre " to suggest rattling bones. This idea gives the best description of its tone. Although it is a tuned instrument and has a compass of about three octaves, it is mostly used for the effect of its strange tone-colour.

Saint-Saens (1835–1921)

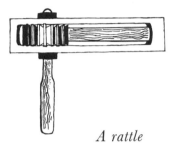

A rattle

Rattle

The rattle used in the orchestra is of the same design as a football rattle. It has been used by Beethoven (as gunfire) in his programme music* " Wellington's Victory ".

Anvil

The anvil used in the orchestra takes its name from the blacksmith's anvil, not because of its shape but because of its sound. The unmistakable sound of the blacksmith's anvil, metal struck by metal, is obtained in the orchestra by hitting steel bars with a special striker. Wagner, in his opera " Rheingold ",

uses eighteen steel bars in three different sizes.

Sometimes unusual noises or effects are required by a composer, and these require special instruments. Our own English composer, Vaughan Williams, uses a wind-machine in his " Sinfonia Antartica ", and the French composer, Satie, asks for a typewriter in a piece called " Parade ".

Wagner (1813–1883)

* Programme music is music which is suggested by or describes a scene, an incident, or perhaps a happening in nature such as a storm.

6. Keyboard Instruments

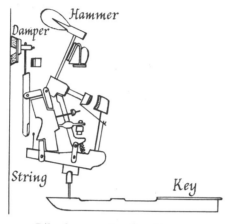

The key-work of a piano

Pianoforte

About 250 years ago in Florence, a man called Cristofori produced what he called a *gravicembalo col piano e forte* (harpsichord with soft and loud). Instead of the strings being plucked, as in the harpsichord, they were hit by small hammers which were worked by the keys when pressed by the fingers. By this means, the degree of loudness and softness of the notes could be controlled by the amount of force the player's fingers used to press the keys.

In order to produce sufficient tone, the top notes of the piano have three strings for each note, the middle notes two, and the lower notes one. These strings are stretched over an iron frame and are fixed at one end to tuning-pins. By means of a special key, the piano-tuner can turn the tuning-pins which bring the strings to their correct pitch. Behind the iron frame is a resonating board, usually made of thin pine, which makes the sound of the piano louder and helps to improve the tone.

After a piano string has been struck by a hammer, it will sound its note for as long as it continues to vibrate. When the finger releases the key a small felt *damper* is made to touch the string, immediately stopping the vibrations, thus causing the sound to cease. Without being " damped " by this piece of felt, the strings would continue to vibrate and the notes of a piece of music would run into each other and blur.

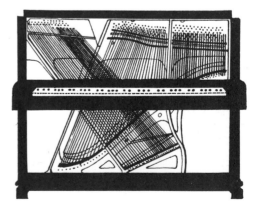

The arrangement of the strings in an upright piano

A grand piano in the orchestra

The right foot-pedal, however, stops the felt from touching the string after it has been struck. By this means, the player can control the length of time the string vibrates. This is a very important means of expression, for in some music the blending—that is mixing—of notes and chords is part of the music's charm and construction.

The left foot-pedal produces a softer sound. This is done in one of two ways : either by moving the hammer a little to one side so that only one or part of the strings is hit, or by altering the angle at which the hammer strikes the string or strings. Apart from these two pedals, all expression and variety of tone are obtained by the way in which the keys are pressed by the fingers.

As a beginner's instrument the piano has one advantage ; all the notes are made for the player. All he has to do is press the keys. To play the violin or oboe the fingers have to be placed in just the right position and the embouchure has to be correct or the notes sound out-of-tune. By having the notes already made, the piano can make the player's ears lazy, and all good musicians should have very sharp ears.

One great advantage of the piano is the way in which it blends well with almost every other instrument. Dance bands, trios (a group of three instruments), orchestras and many other groups all have a use for the piano.

The most famous makes of piano come from Germany. The cost of a piano varies very considerably. Many good second-hand instruments can be bought for £100, whereas a new piano by a famous maker can cost as much as £1000.

Keyboard Instruments

Virginal, Spinet and Harpsichord

From the sixteenth to the eighteenth centuries the virginal, spinet and harpsichord held a similar position to that of the piano today. They might all be thought of as harps placed in wooden cases laid horizontally, with the strings plucked by a plectrum (a small piece of leather or a quill) instead of the fingers. When the key is pressed, it raises the jack in which is fixed the plectrum. This action plucks the metal string, causing it to vibrate. When the key is released the jack falls : this time the plectrum, which is fixed to a movable tongue of wood, slides past the string and the piece of felt touches the string, damping the sound (stopping its vibration).

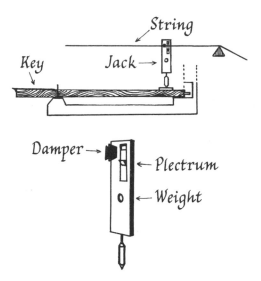

Key-work of virginal, spinet and harpsichord

The virginal is the earliest and simplest member of the harpsichord family. It is shaped like a small oblong box and sometimes placed on a table or a special four-legged stand or frame. Each note has one string made of metal, which produces a pleasant " twang " when plucked.

Apart from light accents, no change of tone or quality is possible by means of touch.

These instruments were made long before concert halls, for use in the intimate atmosphere of the home ; thus their tone is very soft and sweet.

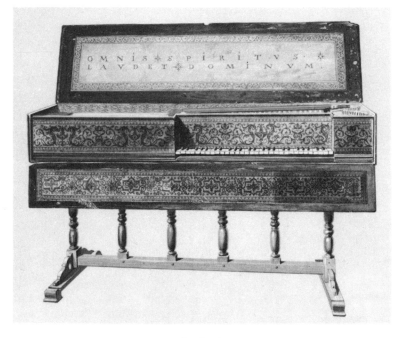

A virginal

66

The spinet is wing-shaped and, like the virginal, has only one string to a note. Its tone is the same as that of the virginal, and Pepys sometimes called the spinet a " triangle virginal ".

Another, but un-familiar, member of the family is the clavi-cytherium. This is a spinet with perpen-dicular strings.

A spinet

The harpsichord is rect-angular in shape with the strings at right angles to the player. Unlike the other earlier instruments it has two strings to each note. Some models were very large, not unlike the modern grand piano in appearance. Extra sets of strings could, by means of stops or levers, be brought in or taken out of use to vary the quantity and quality of the tone. Some instruments possessed a set of strings tuned an octave higher and on rarer occasions an octave lower than the basic group of strings. Two stops often found on these instru-ments imitate the sound of the lute and oboe.

A harpsichord of the eighteenth century

67

Keyboard Instruments

As with the virginal and spinet, finger-touch had little or no effect on the tone of the harpsichord. All the instruments of this group were without a sustaining pedal or a softening pedal. If a key was held down, a note could be sustained for as long as the vibrations lasted.

In 1769 a device called a *Venetian swell* which worked in the same way as a Venetian blind, was added to many instruments. The shutters were placed over the strings and were opened and closed by means of a foot-pedal, thus controlling the volume of tone.

Clavichord

In appearance, the clavichord is like the virginal, but its method of tone production is very different.

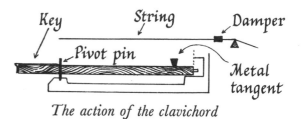

The action of the clavichord

The strings are made to sound by a metal tangent which hits the string and then presses against it. This action not only sets the string in vibration, but because of the pressure of the tangent on the string, determines its pitch by *stopping* the string. The effect of the tangent is the same as that of the player's fingers on a violin. A player can, by holding a key down and rocking his finger, produce a kind of singing tone from the string (remember that the tangent remains in contact with the string after having struck it). This effect prolongs the sound of the note as well as adding a means of expression. On no other stringed keyboard instrument is this effect possible.

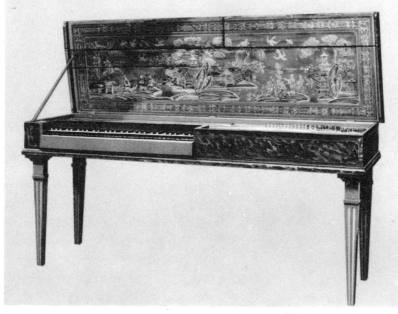

A clavichord

The tone of a clavichord is very soft and beautiful, and, because of its soft quality, is only suitable for solos, and then in a small room. Bach wrote his famous 48 preludes and fugues for this instrument.

Although the harpsichord group of instruments was displaced by the piano, it is well to think of them as different types of instrument. Each has its own legacy of music, which sounds best on the instrument for which it was written. Today, many new harpsicords are being made and they are used in concerts and broadcasts of pre-1700 music. Modern composers have written music for the harpsichord and in general much interest is taken in it.

The skill required to make one is great and the cost is therefore high, perhaps as much as £1000. The old models are even more expensive because of their value as antiques and their particular beauty of tone.

Organ

The organ is the only single musical instrument that varies considerably in size and complexity. It appears to have begun its life as the *pan-pipes* or *syrinx* which originated in Chaldea. As long ago as 516 B.C., the Jews built a large organ in the Second Temple in Jerusalem, and by the tenth century A.D. the art of organ building was well advanced

The portable organ, frequently used for church processions in the fourteenth century, was a simple version of the large organ.

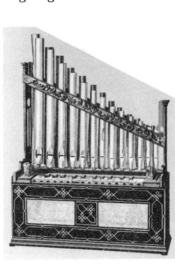

The bellows at the back of the in-strument were worked by the player's right hand.

and a famous organ was built in Winchester Cathedral at this time.

The organ is built up of sets or *ranks* of pipes of different lengths, each pipe sounding one note. These are mounted on a *wind-chest* and are made to sound by wind which is supplied by bellows. Each rank of pipes has its own tone-colour and consists of a complete range of notes.

Pan-pipes

69

Keyboard Instruments

When the player wishes to use a rank of pipes he pulls a *stop* which operates a series of levers attached to a slide. The slide is made of wood in which holes are bored and moves to and fro underneath the tips of the pipes in the wind-chest. The action of pulling the stop moves the slide so that the holes coincide with the tips of the pipes. A small hinged lid, called a *pallet*, which is fitted underneath the tip of each pipe, seals off the supply of air. When the player depresses a key on the keyboard, the pallet, which is connected to the key by a system of rods, moves and allows the wind to sound the pipe.

Each pipe in the organ has its own pallet and set of rods which connect it to the keyboard, each rank of pipes its own wind chest, slide, levers and stop. You can well imagine what a complicated system of rods and levers are required even for a small organ.

Most organs have between two and five keyboards or *manuals* and a pedal keyboard which is a large keyboard made of wood and played by the feet. Each manual has a group of stops associated with it and these can only be operated from that manual. Sometimes each group forms a complete little organ. By means of special stops called *couplers* the different manuals can be coupled together, thus giving a great variety of tone-colour and if necessary a large volume of sound.

The manuals which operate each of the sections or little organs that go to make up the complete organ have the following names (they are grouped in order of importance and, generally speaking, loudness):

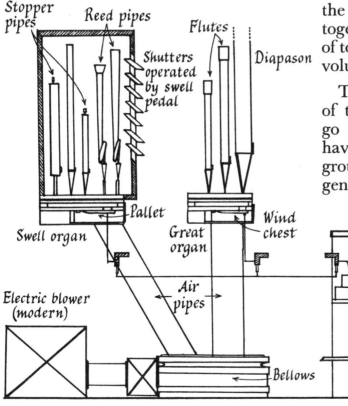

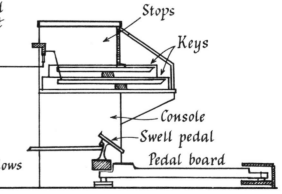

The parts of an organ

The organ in the Royal Festival Hall, London

1.	2.
GREAT ORGAN	SWELL ORGAN
3.	4.
CHOIR ORGAN	SOLO ORGAN
5.	6.
ECHO ORGAN	PEDAL ORGAN

The most important and basic manual is the great organ. It is from this section that the greatest sounds are produced, and all the other manuals can be coupled to it to produce the greatest combination of sound.

The pipes of the swell organ are enclosed in a box fitted with shutters which are opened or closed by a pedal operated by the player's foot. By this method the degree of volume can be controlled. From a very soft sound the tone can be made to swell out, and so the organ is called a swell organ.

The stops on the choir organ are usually of a quieter type, more suited for use with a choir.

On the solo organ the stops are for solo purposes, as the name suggests; many of them have the same name as orchestral instruments, such as flute, oboe or viola. They are imitations of those instruments and sound very much the same.

The echo organ is usually placed away from the main body of the organ in order to give an " echo " or a distant effect. Many of the stops on this organ are of a quiet variety.

Keyboard Instruments

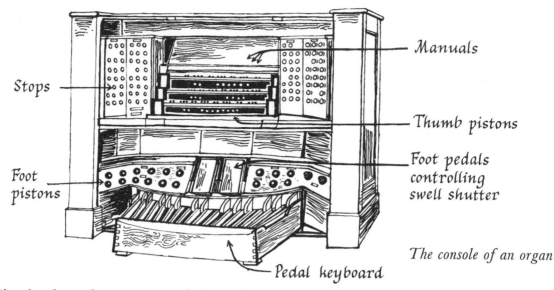

Manuals

Stops

Thumb pistons

Foot pistons

Foot pedals controlling swell shutter

Pedal keyboard

The console of an organ

The keyboards, stops, pedals and other control devices are grouped together in the console, and so arranged that the player can easily work them.

Sometimes the player may instantly require a large number of stops to be pulled out, or vice versa. To do this by hand would take too long and interrupt the flow of the music. By means of small white buttons, called *pistons*, placed just under each manual, and foot pistons placed just above the pedal board, various combinations of stops can be instantly used or changed by the single movement of a foot or thumb.

The picture below shows a console with ivory levers called *rocker-tablets* instead of stops. The function of these tablets is the same as the stops and many players feel they are easier to use. It is important to remember that the organist has to " play " the stops as well as the notes.

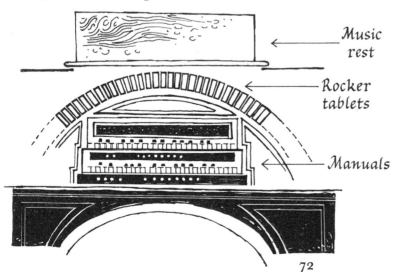

Music rest

Rocker tablets

Manuals

On some organs rocker-tablets are used instead of stops

Most of the pipes are made of wood or metal and are called *flue pipes*, and their sound is produced in the same way as that of the recorder. Others have a specially constructed base in which a thin piece of metal called a *reed* vibrates, producing a note in much the same way as the orchestral reed instruments. These are called reed pipes. The pitch of all the pipes is determined by their length.

Many different kinds of tone-colour can be produced from reed and flue pipes by using different wind pressures, different materials, such as wood or metal, and by differences in scale (this means in diameter). Another way is by using stopped pipes. This is done by inserting a stopper in the top of the pipe. Its effect is to lower the pitch

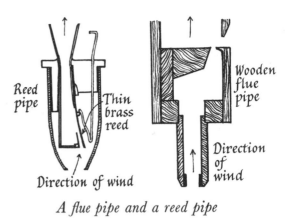

A flue pipe and a reed pipe

of the note an octave as well as give the sound a distinctive quality.

Most organs have a variety of 16-, 8-, 4-, and 2-foot stops. These figures indicate the length of a pipe required to sound the lowest note of a rank of pipes and thc pitch of the notes that all the pipes will sound when the stop is drawn. Many organs also have a number of *mutation stops*; the notes they sound are at different intervals above the 8-foot pitch. The *mixture stops* bring into use a mixture of ranks all at the same time.

The flue stop called the *diapason* gives the basic tone of the organ. With all the different kinds of stops—flutes, diapasons, reed and mutations—not forgetting the couplers, and pedals, you will understand how skilled the organist has to be to play the organ.

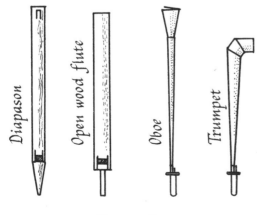

Organ pipes

73

Some Musical Terms to Remember

Clef :

The sign placed at the beginning of the stave from which the name and position of the notes are found. The treble or G clef indicates the position of G.

The bass clef or F clef indicates the position of F.

The C clef indicates the position of middle C. It has two positions and is often called the tenor or alto clef depending on its position.

(The position of pitch of the notes on each clef can be found by relating the notes to middle C.)

Compass :

The range of notes an instrument or voice is able to produce.

Embouchure :

This means the way in which the lips are applied to the mouthpiece of the instrument, or the way in which the lips are used.

Octave :

An octave is an interval of eight notes. An octave below 8va bassa⌟ or higher 8va⌐ means eight notes lower or higher.

Pitch :

The pitch of a note is its position in relation to the other notes of a scale or chord. A note that is off-pitch (out-of-tune) is out of position.

Register :

This word means a section, e.g., the top register of the flute means the top section of the notes a flute can play.

Scale :

An ordered series or group of notes played or sung in steps.

Stave :

The lines and spaces on which the notes of music are written.

Tone-colour :

This expression is used to describe the sound or tone an instrument produces.

Musical Forms

All music is arranged in a musical pattern or form. Here are the meanings of some of the musical forms mentioned in this book.

Cantata : A composition using voices, often with orchestral or instrumental accompaniment, the subject of which may be sacred or secular.

Concerto : This is an Italian word which means a " concert ". When used as the title of a composition it means a work for a solo instrument and orchestra written in Symphonic form, usually without the Minuet movement.

Fugue : Works written in this form consist of a set number of voices or musical strands woven together in a certain way. At the beginning the subject or theme of the Fugue is played by one voice, after which each of the other voices enters in turn with the same subject. The subject usually forms the basis from which the rest of the composition is developed.

Serenade : As a musical form it indicates an instrumental composition containing several movements of varying character. Usually it is less serious in content than a symphony.

Symphony : Literally the word means " sounding together ". In the seventeenth century it was often used instead of the word Overture. Today it is accepted as meaning a composition for orchestra in four movements : First Movement—Slow Movement—Minuet and Trio—Finale. Many composers have written symphonies that do not keep strictly to this form, e.g., Sibelius, Symphony No. 7.

Suite : A set of movements in various dance forms. In early Suites the principal dance forms used were : Allemande, Courante, Sarabande and Gigue. These were often preceded by a Prelude. On occasions a Bourree, Gavotte or Minuet was introduced. The modern Suite does not always use dance forms : instead, contrast is obtained by the use of different keys (the movements of the older Suites were usually in the same key), tempi, and character for each movement.

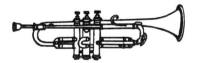

Musical Works to Illustrate the Different Instruments with Suggested Recordings

The recordings suggested here are intended as a guide to those who want to learn more about the sound of the different instruments. Wherever possible, good cheap recordings have been suggested.

	Instruments of the Orchestra: *with a commentary by Sir Adrian Boult*	MFP 2092
RECORDER	*Vivaldi* Concerto in C	H 71022
FLUTE	*Bach* Suite No. 2 in B minor	ASD 404–5
	Debussy A l'après-midi d'un faune	XLP 30092
	Mozart Flute Concerto No. 1 in G major K.313	SAL 3499
PICCOLO	*Beethoven* Egmont Overture	ECS 556
	Brahms Variations on a theme by Haydn	SAX 2424
	Vivaldi Piccolo Concerto in C major	SAW 9426
OBOE	*Martinu* Oboe Concerto	SUA 10486
	Mozart Oboe Concerto	(DGG) 135069
COR ANGLAIS	*Dvorak* New World Symphony (slow movement)	SAX 2405
	Franck Symphony in D minor (slow movement)	SXLP 30055
	Sibelius The Swan of Tuonela: from Four Legends	ASD 2308
OBOE D'AMORE	*Bach* Et in spiritum: from Mass in B minor	(DGG) 2710001
CLARINET	*Brahms* Symphony No. 1 (third movement)	XLP 30023
	Mozart Clarinet Concerto	ASD 344
BASSOON	*Brahms* Piano Concerto No. 1 (opening of slow movement)	SXL 6023
	Mozart Bassoon Concerto	ASD 344
SAXOPHONE	*Bizet* L'Arlesienne Suites: Suite No. 1 (second movement), Suite No. 2 (third movement)	HQS 1108
HORN	*Beethoven* Symphony No. 3 (trio from the scherzo)	ECS 535
	Handel Water Music	ASD 577 or 6500 047
	Mozart Horn Concerto in E flat, K.447	SAX 2406
TRUMPET	*Dvorak* New World Symphony (last movement)	SAX 2405
	Handel Aria—The Trumpet Shall Sound: from Messiah	SAL 3623
	Haydn Trumpet Concerto	ZRG 543

TROMBONE	*Beethoven* Symphony No. 5 (last movement)	ECS 518
	Mozart The Magic Flute (overture)	SAN 137
TUBA	*Brahms* Symphony No. 2	HQS 1143
	Brahms Tragic Overture	ECS 520
CORNET	*Franck* Symphony in D minor	SXLP 30055
VIOLIN & VIOLA	*Mendelssohn* Violin Concerto in E minor	MAL 714
	Mozart Symphonie Concertante in E flat, K.364	SAL 3492
		or SXLP20112
'CELLO	*Haydn* 'Cello Concerto in D	UN 5207
	Saint-Saens The Swan: from Carnival of the Animals	72072
	Schumann 'Cello Concerto	138674
DOUBLE BASS	*Dittersdorf* Double Bass Concerto	TV 34005S
	Dvorak New World Symphony (the last two chords of the second movement)	SAX 2405
	Sibelius Symphony No. 2 (opening of second movement)	SDD 234
VIOLA DA GAMBA	*Bach* Brandenburg Concerto No. 6	135116
VIOLA D'AMORE	*Vivaldi* Viola d'Amore Concerto in D minor	TV 34009S
HARP	*Bizet* L'Arlesienne Suites	HQS 1108
	Dittersdorf Harp Concerto	TV 34005S
HARPSICHORD	*Handel & Couperin* Harpsichord music	HQS1085
TYMPANI	*Brahms* Symphony No. 4 (opening of last movement)	138927
	Elgar Enigma Variations (seventh variation)	GSGC 14057
	Mozart Serenade No. 6	135126
	Sibelius Symphony No. 1 (the opening and final bars)	GSGC 14058
CELESTA	*Tchaikovsky* Dance of the Sugar Plum Fairy: from Nutcracker Suite	SDD 150
PIANO	*Bartok* Piano Concerto No. 3	ASD 2476
	Prokofiev Piano Concerto No. 3	ASD 2701
	Beethoven Piano Concerto No. 4	TV 34208
	Mozart Piano Concerto No. 24	136196
ORGAN	*Bach* Toccata and Fugue in D minor; Fantasia and Fugue in G minor; Two Chorale Preludes; Toccata Adagio and Fugue in C major; Fugue in G major; Prelude and Fugue in A minor	ECS 528

The Following Works Illustrate Different Groups of Instruments

FLUTE AND HARP *Mozart* Concerto for flute and harp in C major — ST 935

TRUMPET, FLUTE, OBOE AND VIOLIN
Bach Brandenburg Concerto No. 2 — MAL 669

OBOE, BASSOON, VIOLIN AND 'CELLO
Haydn Symphonie Concertante in B flat — H 71024

OBOES, CLARINETS, BASSOONS, CONTRA BASSOON, HORNS, 'CELLO AND DOUBLE BASS
Dvorak Serenade in D minor — SLPEM 136481

WOOD-WIND AND TROMBONE
Mozart The Magic Flute (Overture) — SAN 137

HORNS, TROMBONES AND TUBA
Humperdinck Hansel and Gretel (Prelude) — OC 187

WOOD-WIND AND BRASS, WITH BASS CLARINET
Franck Symphony in D minor — SXLP 30055

DOUBLE BASS AND VIOLA
Dittersdorf Sinfonia Concertante in D major — TV 34005S

STRING ORCHESTRA AND STRING QUARTET
Elgar Introduction and Allegro for Strings — ASD 521

LUTE AND VIOLA D'AMORE
Vivaldi Concerto for lute and viola d'amore in D minor — TV 34009S

LUTE, VIOLA DA GAMBA AND VIOLA D'AMORE
Bach St. John Passion, 31, 32, 58 — SAWT 9479

Miscellaneous Recordings of Interest

Prokofiev	Peter and the Wolf	ACL 30
Stravinsky	Petroushka	ECM 508
Roussel	Le Festin de l'Araignée; Petite Suite	ACL 270
Schubert	Symphony No. 9, "The Great"	ACL 70

Books about Music and Musicians

Boyhoods of Great Composers, Books 1 and 2 by Catherine Gough (O.U.P.)

Mozart by Irene Gass (A. & C. Black)

Great Musicians' Series by Opal Wheeler and Sybil Deucher (Faber)
Separate books on Bach, Beethoven, Brahms, Chopin (2), Stephen Foster, Grieg, Handel, Haydn, Mozart, Paganini, Schubert, Schumann, Tchaikovsky (2) and Wagner.

The Orchestra by Mervyn Bruxner (O.U.P.)

I Want to be a Musician by Carla Greene (Chambers)

Great Performers by Pat Young (O.U.P.)

Music by Percy M. Young (Nelson)

Let's Make an Opera by Eric Crozier (O.U.P.)

The Golden Cockerel by Enid Gibson (O.U.P.)

The Sorcerer's Apprentice and Other Stories by Enid Gibson (O.U.P.)

FOR OLDER BOYS AND GIRLS

Introducing Music by Otto Karolyi (Penguin)

Young Person's Guide to Concerts by Michael Hurd (Routledge)

The Listener's Guide to Music by Percy A. Scholes (O.U.P.)

The Concerto by Ralph Hill (Penguin)

A New Dictionary of Music by Arthur Jacobs (Penguin)

The Pelican History of Music, Books 1, 2, 3 (Penguin)

Making Music by Nicholas Fiske (Michael Joseph)

Keys to the Keyboard : A Book for Pianists by Andor Foldes (O.U.P.)

Separate volumes on *Flute Technique, Oboe Technique, Clarinet Technique, Bassoon Technique, Horn Technique, Trumpet Technique, Recorder Technique, Orchestral Percussion Technique*, all by well-known performers (O.U.P.)

Index

(The numbers refer to the pages of the book. Numbers like this—*16*—refer to pages on which there are main entries.)

80